Low-Fat Vegan Recipes

125 Fast and Easy Low-Fat Vegan Recipes to Excite Your Taste Buds

By Lora Campbell

Low-Fat Vegan Recipes

Printed in the United States of America.
First Printing, 2013

Table of Contents

Introduction

The Vegan lifestyle is not just popular among people wanting to lose weight. In fact, most people that choose to eat a Vegan diet make that decision because they have strong convictions about not eating animals or animal byproducts. If you want to adhere to a true Vegan lifestyle, that means your diet will have no meat or dairy.

While eating a Vegan diet is increasingly common, it still can pose some challenges to your everyday life, so I have a simple solution for you. Now you can quickly and easily enjoy tasty Vegan-friendly soups, stews, salads, appetizers, snacks, breakfasts, side dishes, main dishes, deserts, sauces and dressings. Everything you need to eat healthy Vegan meals that taste delicious.

In this cookbook, you will find 125 Vegan recipes that are low-fat and convenient. None of these recipes take more than 30 minutes to prepare. A few will require longer cooking times in a slow cooker, but only 30 minutes of prep time will be needed.

If you want a shortcut to yummy, nutritious Vegan meals, turn the page and get started on your first low-fat Vegan delicacy!

Sweet Potato Pear Soup

Ingredients:

1 TBSP vegan margarine
1 small onion, chopped
1/4 cup chopped carrot
1/4 cup chopped celery
3 sweet potatoes, peeled and diced
2 pears, cored, peeled, and diced
1/2 tsp thyme
1 tsp paprika
5 cups vegetable broth
1/3 cup coconut milk
2 tsp maple syrup
Juice from ½ lemon
Salt and pepper to taste

Directions:

In a large soup pot, heat margarine and sauté onion, carrot, and celery over medium heat. After one minute, add in sweet potatoes, pears, and thyme and bring to a boil Simmer for 15 minutes or until the sweet potatoes are cooked through. Pour the mixture into a blender and puree until smooth.

Return to the pot and add coconut milk, maple syrup, and juice from your lime. Simmer for 5-10 minutes. Season with salt and pepper to taste.

Carrot and Ginger Harvest Soup

Ingredients:

1 TBSP olive oil
1 small onion, diced
2 garlic cloves, minced
2 TBSP fresh grated ginger
1 large apple, peeled, cored, and chopped
5 large carrots, peeled and chopped
4 cups vegetable broth
½ tsp nutmeg
Salt and pepper to taste

Directions:

In a large soup pot, heat olive oil and sauté onion over medium heat. Add in minced garlic and ginger and cook for two minutes. Next, add your apples and carrots and allow to cook for two more minutes. Stir in your vegetable broth and bring to a boil. Reduce heat and simmer for half an hour or until the carrots and apples are tender. Pour your mixture into a blender and puree until smooth. Then season with nutmeg, salt, and pepper to taste.

White Bean Soup

Ingredients:

5 cups cooked white beans
1 ½ TBSP olive oil
1 yellow onion, chopped
1 carrot, chopped
1 stalk of celery, chopped
3 Rome tomatoes, chopped
3 cloves garlic, minced
1/2 tsp thyme
2 cups water
1/2 tsp dried basil
Salt and Pepper to taste

Directions:

In a large soup pot, heat olive oil and sauté onions until translucent. Add in carrots and celery and cook for five minutes. Then stir in tomatoes and your spices. Allow to simmer for 5 minutes. While you wait, puree four cups of (precooked!) beans in a blender. Then stir in the pureed beans along with the cup of whole cooked beans into the soup. Stir it all together and all to simmer for 20 minutes. Add more salt and pepper as needed.

Pumpkin Tofu Chowder

Ingredients:

1/2 cup pumpkin purée
1 medium potato, peeled and diced
2 cloves garlic, minced
1 cup corn
1 1/2 cups tofu, cubed
1 tsp thyme
1 tsp parley
1 TBSP vegan bouillon
4 cups water
1 cup unsweetened almond milk
Cayenne pepper to taste
Salt and pepper to taste

Directions:

This recipe is best prepared in a slow cooker so it can simmer on low all day. Put all the ingredients except almond milk in the slow cooker and stir together to combine. Cover and cook on low for 6-8 hours. Stir in the almond milk and add extra salt and pepper as needed. Cook for 30 more minutes and then serve warm.

Fat Blaster Cabbage Soup

Ingredients:

2 yellow onions, diced
5 cloves of garlic, minced
1 cup sliced mushrooms
6 stalks celery, chopped
4 carrots, peeled and chopped
½ head of green cabbage, shredded
2 cans (16 oz) diced tomatoes
10 cups vegetable broth
1 tsp thyme
Salt and Pepper to taste

Directions:

In a large soup pot, sauté onion, garlic, and mushrooms in 3 cups of vegetable broth until onions are translucent. Stir in the remaining ingredients and bring to a boil. Turn down the heat to low and simmer for two hours or until all the vegetables are tender. Add salt and pepper to taste.

Snow Day Vegan Chili

Ingredients:

1 large yellow onion, chopped
2 TBSP olive oil
3 cloves garlic, minced
1 chipotle chile in adobo sauce, drained and minced
1 cup chopped mushrooms
3 carrots, peeled and chopped
3 cups seitan, chopped
3 TBSP tomato paste
2 tsp paprika
2 tsp oregano
1 ½ tsp chili powder
¾ tsp celery salt
2 TBSP Vegan soy sauce
1 TBSP Vegan Worcestershire sauce
1 can each: chili beans, black beans, pinto beans

Directions:

In a large pot, sauté onions over medium heat until translucent. Add in mushrooms, garlic and chile and continue cooking for four minutes. Add in seitan, tomato pace, and spices and 1 cup of water.

Cook three more minutes, stirring. Add all the beans, carrots, soy sauce, and Worcestershire sauce. Cover with a lid and simmer for one hour on low heat.

Chilled Cantaloupe Soup

Ingredients:

1 large cantaloupe, peeled, and cut into cubes
1/3 cup orange juice
4 lime wedges

Directions:

In a blender, combine cantaloupe and orange juice and puree until smooth. Pour into bowls and chill for at least one hour. Squeeze with a lime wedge before serving.

Red Lentil Pumpkin Soup

Ingredients:

3 TBSP coconut oil
1 cup red lentils
6 cups vegetable broth
1 cup pumpkin puree
2 small onions, chopped
1 cup baby spinach leaves
2 TBSP grated ginger
4 cloves garlic, minced
Salt and pepper to taste

Directions:

In a large pot, heat coconut oil over medium heat until melted. Add in remaining ingredients except spinach leaves and bring to a boil. Turn down the heat and simmer on low-medium for 45 minutes or until lentils are soft. Add spinach leaves and cook 5-10 more minutes or until spinach wilts. Serve warm.

Cuban Black Bean Soup

Ingredients:

2 tsp olive oil
1 yellow onion, diced
1 red bell pepper, seeded and diced
1 green bell pepper, seeded and diced
6 cups black beans, cooked
6 cloves garlic, chopped
3 medium potatoes, peeled and diced
1 TBSP cumin
1 TBSP oregano
2 tsp parsley
1 tsp salt
½ tsp pepper
2 TBSP white wine vinegar

Directions:

In a large pot, sauté onion, peppers, and garlic in olive oil for 3 minutes. Pour the mixture in a blender along with 3 cups of beans and 6 cups of water. Puree until smooth. Pour the mixture back into the pot and add in the rest of the beans, potatoes, vinegar, and seasonings. Continue cooking for 30 minutes or until potatoes are soft.

Slow Cooker Indian Chickpea Soup

Ingredients:

1 pound split chickpeas (dal)
2 medium onions, diced
6 cloves of garlic, minced
1 TBSP ginger, minced
1 can (15 oz) diced tomatoes
4 cups low sodium vegetable broth
2 TBSP cumin
2 tsp coriander
¼ tsp turmeric
2 tsp black mustard seeds
3 cups mixed frozen vegetables
1/2 bunch of cilantro, chopped

Directions:

Rinse chickpeas and drain. Place all ingredients in the slow cooker except for frozen vegetables and cook on low for 10 hours. You can also cook overnight if desired. When the chickpeas are soft and begin breaking apart, stir in vegetables and any additional seasonings desired and continue cooking for 30 minutes. Garnish with cilantro on top.

Garden Tea Soup

Ingredients:

2 cups boiling water
2 Green Tea Bags
1 TBSP olive oil
4 cloves garlic
1 tsp thyme
1 bay leaf
4 cups vegetable broth
1 ½ cups mixed vegetables (frozen)
½ cup rice
½ tsp salt
Juice from ½ lemon

Directions:

Brew tea bags in boiling water for 2 minutes. While the tea steeps, heat olive oil in a large pot and sauté garlic, thyme, and bay leaf. Pour in broth, brewed tea, and mixed vegetables. Bring to a boil and stir in rice and salt. Reduce heat to low and cover. Simmer for 20 minutes or until rice is cooked and tender. Remove the bay leaf and garlic cloves and spritz with lemon juice. Serve warm.

Garlic Potato Soup

Ingredients:

4 cloves of garlic, minced
6 red potatoes, sliced
2 large red onions, chopped
7 cups vegetable broth
Salt and pepper to taste

Directions:

In a large soup pot, boil potatoes until soft. Drain and stir in vegetable broth and onions. Add in garlic, salt, and pepper and simmer for 30 minutes over low heat to combine flavors. Use a potato masher to break apart potato chunks or use a blender to puree for a smoother consistency. Sprinkle parsley on top and serve warm.

Tomato Gazpacho Soup

Ingredients:

3 large tomatoes
1 cucumber, peeled and chopped
1 large red pepper, chopped
1/4 red onion, diced
1 cup fresh basil, chopped
4 cloves fresh garlic, minced
½ small green chili pepper
1 tsp salt
¼ cup water
2 TBSP olive oil
Juice from 1 lemon
2 TBSP agave nectar

Directions:

Place all ingredients in a large pot and bring to a boil. Cook for 20 minutes over medium heat. Pour the whole mixture into a blender and pulse until smooth. Serve warm with basil on top for a garnish.

Vegan Minestrone Soup

Ingredients:

1 large onion, chopped
2 Carrots, chopped
6 cups Vegetable Broth
3 Zucchini, cut into matchsticks
4 stalks Celery, chopped
1 TBSP Basil
1 TBSP Oregano
2 tsp Rosemary
½ tsp Salt
½ tsp Black Pepper
4 cups grape tomatoes, halved
4 cloves Garlic, minced
2 cups rigatoni pasta
3 cups cooked navy beans

Directions:

In a large soup pot, sauté carrots and onions over medium heat for 3 minutes. Add a small amount of water. Stir in the remaining ingredients except for beans. Bring to a boil, then reduce heat to low and cover. Simmer for 10 minutes or until pasta is tender. Stir in your cooked beans and continue cooking until they are warmed through.

Asparagus Lemon Twist Soup

Ingredients:

3 TBSP olive oil
2 large leeks, sliced
5 large red potatoes, chopped
15-20 stalks of asparagus, trimmed and chopped
8 cups vegetable broth
Juice of 2 lemons
Salt and pepper to taste

Directions:

In a large soup pot, sauté the leeks in olive oil until soft and translucent. Add the potatoes and vegetable broth and bring to a boil. Cook until potatoes are tender. Add in the asparagus and blanch for 2-3 minutes or until tender. Pour mixture into a blender and puree until smooth. Pour in fresh lemon juice gradually and continue to pulse to mix well. Serve warm with an extra lemon wedge for garnish.

Cranberry Broccoli Salad

Ingredients:

1 small head of broccoli cut into small florets
3 cups baby spinach
2 cups romaine lettuce
1 8 oz. package sugar snap peas
1 apple peeled and sliced into match sticks
2 small seedless cucumbers, sliced
1 cup plum tomatoes, sliced
1 large avocado, peeled and chopped
2 green onions, chopped
3 TBSP dried cranberries
Juice from 3 oranges
2 TBSP olive oil
Salt and pepper to taste

Directions:

Combine all ingredients in a bowl and toss well to combine. Chill for 30 minutes before serving.

Vegan Curried Potato Salad

Ingredients:

1 ½ cups silken tofu
¼ cup chia gel (2 TBSP chia seeds mixed with ¼ cup cold water)
¼ cup olive oil
1 tsp mustard
1 ½ tsp curry powder
½ tsp cumin
½ tsp cayenne
12 red skinned potatoes, boiled and cubed (cooled)
1 red onion, chopped
½ green bell pepper, chopped
½ red bell pepper, chopped
1 Serrano chili pepper, minced
1/2 bunch parsley, chopped
1 cup celery, finely chopped
Salt to taste

Directions:

In a food processor, blend together olive oil, tofu, chia gel, mustard, and spices. Once the mixture is smooth, pour into a bowl and toss to combine with remaining ingredients. Refrigerate for 30 minutes before serving.

Eggless Vegan Egg Salad

Ingredients:

1 pound firm tofu, patted dry
½ cup low fat soy mayo
Juice from ½ lemon
1 tsp dried onion
¾ tsp garlic
½ tsp salt
¼ tsp turmeric
1/8 tsp pepper
½ cup carrots, shredded
½ cup red bell pepper, diced
½ cup celery, diced
¼ cup chives, chopped
¼ cup parsley, chopped

Directions:

Squeeze moisture out of tofu by pressing over a colander. Crumbled the pressed tofu in a large bowl. Add in remaining ingredients and stir well to combine. Cover and chill for at least 1 hour before serving.

5-Minute Red Cabbage Salad

Ingredients:

½ head of red cabbage
2 bunches of flat leaf Italian parsley
Juice of 2 lemons
½ cup olive oil
8 chives
Salt and pepper to taste

Directions:

Place the cabbage, parsley, and onions into a food processor and pulse just a few times to get a rough chop. Toss the mixture with olive oil and lemon and season to taste.

Cucumber Seaweed Salad

Ingredients:

4 cups cut wakame, soaked, rinsed, and drained
2 cups cucumber, julienned
3 TBSP tamari
4 TBSP rice vinegar
2 TBSP sesame oil
Juice from ½ lemon
2 tsp minced ginger
2 tsp agave nectar

Directions:

Mix seaweed and cucumber in a big bowl. Place remaining ingredients in a blender and pulse until well combined. Pour mixture over the seaweed and cucumber and toss. Garnish with sesame seeds if desired.

Hot and Spicy Carrot Salad

Ingredients:

4 cups grated carrots
½ cup raisins
Juice from 2 lemons
2 TBSP red wine vinegar
2 TBSP water
¼ tsp paprika
¼ tsp cumin
¼ tsp cayenne
½ cup cilantro

Directions:

Boil raisings until plump. Mix together with remaining ingredients and toss to combine. Chill for 30 minutes before servings.

Spinach Pear Salad

Ingredients:

3 cups spinach leaves
1 pear, diced to ½ inch pieces
1/3 cup pomegranate seeds
1/8 tsp pepper
3 TBSP balsamic vinegar

Directions:

Toss the pear slices with vinegar and pepper. Pour mixture over spinach in a salad bowl and top with pomegranate seeds.

Strawberry Pecan Salad

Ingredients:

2 cups baby spinach leaves
2 cups of strawberries, capped and sliced
1 red onion, diced
1/3 cup pecans, chopped
¼ cup mandarin orange juice
4 small dates, pitted
2 tsp apple cider vinegar
1 tsp chia seeds

Directions:

Combine all ingredients in a large salad bowl and toss to combine. Chill for 30 minutes before serving.

Thai Hot and Sour Salad

Ingredients:

2 red chilies, deseeded
2 cloves garlic
4 TBSP soy sauce
Juice from 1 lime
4 TBSP splenda
8 oz. baked tofu, cut into bite size pieces
11 oz. grated rutabaga
2/3 cup green beans, sliced
1 red bell pepper, julienned
4 chives, chopped
2 handfuls mint leaves
½ cup toasted peanuts, chopped

Directions:

Combine all ingredients in a large salad bowl and toss well to combine. Serve immediately.

Three Bean Salad

Ingredients:

1 can green beans, drained
1 can wax beans, drained
1 can kidney beans, drained
1 green bell pepper, chopped
2/3 cup apple juice
1/3 cup apple cider vinegar
2 tsp sugar
½ tsp pepper
¼ tsp dry mustard
¼ tsp paprika
1/8 tsp oregano

Directions:

Combine beans with bell pepper in a large bowl and toss to combine. In a small bowl, stir together the remaining ingredients to create a vinaigrette dressing. Pour over salad and toss gently. Cover and chill for 2 hours before serving.

Summer Watermelon Salad

Ingredients:

4 cups watermelon, cut in 1/2-inch cubes
1/2 cup diced red onion
4 TBSP rice vinegar
2 TBSP chopped fresh mint
1/2 tsp pepper

Directions:

Combine all ingredients in a large bowl and toss to combine. Serve immediately.

Roasted Beet Hummus

Ingredients:

3 medium beets, roasted, peeled then cut into
2 TBSP tahini
1/4 cup lemon juice
1 clove garlic, chopped
1/4 cup olive oil
Salt to taste

Directions:

Process all ingredients in a food processor. Blend until smooth. Serve with a hefty drizzle of olive oil.

Simple Blender Applesauce

Ingredients:

3 medium apples, peeled and cored
1 banana
1 date, pitted
1/2 cup water
1 tsp cinnamon
dash of allspice

Directions:

Place the apples, water, banana, cinnamon and allspice in a blender and pulse until pureed. If you use a frozen banana, it creates a better consistency.

Vegan Bruschetta

Ingredients:

2 TBSP Olive Oil
5 cloves Garlic, minced
1 pint grape tomatoes, halved
1 pint Yellow Grape Tomatoes, halved
1 TBSP Balsamic Vinegar
1 TBSP basil
Salt and Pepper to taste

Directions:

Over medium heat, sauté garlic until golden brown. Transfer to a mixing bowl and stir in remaining ingredients. Toss to combine and adjust seasoning as needed. Refrigerate for an hour before serving.

Chocolate Banana Snack Shake

Ingredients:

2 ripe bananas
1/4 cup water
1 TBSP cocoa powder
handful of ice cubes
2 TBSP honey

Directions:

Place all the ingredients in a blender and pulse until smooth.

Zucchini Fritters

Ingredients:

2 zucchini, shredded and squeezed to remove moisture
½ yellow onion, diced
4 cloves garlic, minced
1-½ cups bread crumbs
2 vegan egg replacers
1 tsp baking powder
Salt and Pepper to taste

Directions:

Preheat oven to 350 degrees. In a mixing bowl, combine all ingredients except 1 cup of bread crumbs. Pour that last cup into a shallow dish and reserve. Using your hands to make medium sized patties about 3-4 inches wide. Dip the patties in the reserved bread crumbs to completely cover each side. Then place on a greased baking sheet. Bake the fritters for 40 minutes, turning once to insure even browning on both sides.

Baked Garlic Fries

Ingredients:

3 cloves garlic cloves, minced
2 TBSP olive oil
3 russet potatoes
½ tsp salt
1 TBSP chopped flat leaf parsley

Directions:

Preheat the oven to 450 degrees. Slice potatoes into ¼ inch sticks. Then toss in a bowl of olive oil and garlic. Sprinkle with salt and parsley and bake for 25-35 minutes.

Jicama with Red Chile and Lime

Ingredients:

1 medium jicama
3 oranges, peeled and cut into ¼ inch slices
2 cucumbers, peeled and thinly sliced
Juice from 1 lime
2 tsp chili powder
1/3 cup chopped cilantro
Salt and pepper

Directions:

Cut jicama into 1/4-inch-thick slices. Combine jicama, oranges, cucumbers, radishes, and juice in a bowl and allow it to sit for 30 minutes undisturbed. Add remaining ingredients and mix well.

Persimmon Fruit Pudding

Ingredients:

2 persimmons, very ripe
1 banana
2 TBSP raisins
Coconut shavings

Directions:

Slice persimmons in half and remove insides. Place the flesh into a blender along with banana. Puree until smooth. Top with raisins and coconut and serve immediately or refrigerate.

Pickled Jalapenos

Ingredients:

8 jalapenos, cut into 1/4-inch slices
2 medium carrots, cut into 1/4-inch rounds
1 1/2 cups apple cider vinegar
2 bay leaves
2 tsp salt
1 tsp brown sugar
1/4 tsp whole black peppercorns

Directions:

In a medium pot, combine carrots, vinegar, 2 cups water, bay leaves, salt, sugar, and peppercorns. Bring to a boil and then reduce heat and simmer for 2 minutes. Place jalapenos in a heat safe bowl and then pour the mixture on top. Allow it the jalapenos to sit in the mixture for at least one hour.

Pumpkin Pie Dip with Apple Slices

Ingredients:

½ cup golden raisins
8 dried dates, pitted and chopped
¼ cup unsweetened almond milk
1½ small gala apples, peeled and chopped
1 can pumpkin purée
2 TBSP almond butter
2 tsp pumpkin pie spice
1 tsp apple cider vinegar
8 apples, unpeeled, for dipping (I love Honeycrisp)
Pineapple Juice

Directions:

Place raisins in a small bowl and cover with water. Microwave for 1 minute and then drain. Place the plumped raisins, dates, and almond milk in a food processor and pulse until it is all broken into small pieces. Add in chopped apple and continue pulsing until mixture is similar to a chutney. Add the pumpkin puree, almond butter, pumpkin pie spice, and vinegar. Pulse for about 3-4 minutes or until the mixture is smooth. Slice the 8 apples for soak in pineapple juice to prevent browning. Serve the dip surrounded by apple slices for a delicious fall treat.

Berry Cashew Cream Parfait

Ingredients:

1 cup walnuts, roughly chopped
1 cup raw cashews
½ cup water
2 TBSP agave nectar
1 tsp vanilla extract
pinch of salt
½ cup blueberries
½ cup raspberries

Directions:

Combine cashews, water, agave nectar, vanilla, and salt in a blender. Pulse to combine until puree is smooth and creamy. In a large glass, layer cashew crew, berries, and walnuts, then repeat until you reach the top of the glass.

Southwest Sweet Potato Hash

Ingredients:

1/2 red onion, diced
3 cloves of garlic, minced
1 bell pepper, diced
2 cups cooked black beans
3 cups cooked red quinoa
1/2 bunch cilantro, chopped
2 green onions, sliced
2 TBSP Balsamic vinegar
2 tsp cumin
2 tsp paprika
4 tsp soy sauce
1-2 large kale leaves, chopped
1 large yam, baked and cubed
chili powder to taste
Salt and pepper to taste
1 small Avocado, chopped

Directions:

Sauté onions over medium heat for 3-4 minutes. Add in garlic and bell peppers and sauté for 2 more minutes. Stir in black beans and quinoa and continue cooking for 3 minutes. Add seasonings and kale.

Cook just until the kale start to wilt, then add green onions, cilantro, and yam pieces. When the whole mixture is hot and well blended, spoon into bowls and top with avocado.

Easy Breakfast Potatoes

Ingredients:

4 potatoes, peeled and sliced into thin rounds
½ green bell pepper, sliced
½ red bell pepper, sliced
½ yellow onion, chopped
1 clove garlic, minced
1 tsp basil
1 tsp parsley
1/8 tsp cayenne
1 tsp crushed red pepper
Salt and pepper to taste
2 tsp Olive oil

Directions:

Place the potatoes, onions and peppers in skillet with a thin layer of olive oil coating the bottom. Add in your spices and herbs. Cover and cook for about an hour on medium heat. When they are completely tender and your home smells like heaven, they are ready to enjoy.

Breakfast Cookies

Ingredients:

1/4 cup brown sugar
1/4 cup agave nectar
1/4 cup almond milk
1/4 cup vegan margarine
1 cup silken tofu
1 TBSP vanilla
1 banana
2 cups whole wheat flour
1 tsp baking powder
1/4 tsp salt
1 tsp cinnamon
1 cup steel cut oats
1 apple
1 cup shredded carrots
1 cup chopped pecans

Directions:

Combine all ingredients together and mix well to combine. The battery will be a thick creamy consistency. Drop by spoonfuls on a greased cookie sheet and bake for 14 minutes at 350 degrees.

White Chocolate Citrus Muffins

Ingredients:

1/4 cup agave nectar
1/4 cup almond milk
Zest from ½ orange
Juice from 1 orange
1 tsp balsamic vinegar
2 TBSP applesauce
¼ cup vegan white chocolate chips
¼ tsp salt
½ cup plus 2 TBSP whole wheat flour
½ cup plus 2 TBSP cornmeal
½ tsp baking soda

Directions:

Preheat oven to 350 degrees. Combine all ingredients and stir until well combined. Pour batter into lined muffin tin. Bake for 18-20 minutes or until golden brown.

Scrambled Tofu

Ingredients:

1/4 cup cashews
1 pound tofu, extra firm
1/2 tsp salt
1/4 tsp garlic powder
2 TBSP chopped chives
4 tsp vegetable broth powder
1/2 teaspoon onion powder
2 tsp nutritional yeast
1/4 teaspoon turmeric
1 green bell pepper, chopped
1 yellow onion, chopped
1/2 cup water

Directions:

Drain tofu thoroughly. Soak cashews in ½ cup water for five minutes and then add in salt, garlic powder, vegetable broth powder, onion powder, yeast, and turmeric. Next, sauté the onions, peppers, and chives in a skillet. Then crumble the tofu in the pan and pour the cashew mixture on top. Mix well and heat until all the flavors are well blended.

Banana Chocolate Chip Muffins

Ingredients:

1 cup gluten free flour mix
½ cup agave nectar
½ cup vegan chocolate chips
1 tsp xanthan
1 tsp baking powder
¾ tsp salt
¾ tsp baking soda
1 cup almond milk
1/3 cup canola oil
1 banana
2 tsp apple cider vinegar
1 tsp vanilla extract
½ tsp almond extract

Directions:

Preheat oven to 350 degrees. Mix together all ingredients with an electric mixer until well combined. Pour into a lined muffin pan and cook for 17-20 minutes. Allow to rest and cool at least half an hour before eating.

Strawberry Breakfast Syrup

Ingredients:

1 cup strawberry jam
1/4 cup non-dairy butter
2 tsp light brown sugar
Zest from ½ orange

Directions:

In a small saucepan, heat together all ingredients and stir until smooth. Serve over vegan-friendly pancakes or waffles.

Vegan French Toast

Ingredients:

2-3 ripe bananas
3/4 cup almond milk
1 1/2 tsp cinnamon
1 tsp pumpkin pie spice
1 tsp vanilla extract
Bread, any kind is fine
Vegan margarine

Directions:

In a blender, combine bananas, almond milk, cinnamon, pumpkin pie spice, and vanilla. Puree until smooth. Pour mixture into a wide pie plate and dip bread slices in the mix coating on both sides. Heat some vegan margarine in a plan and then brown the bread on both sides.

Pumpkin Raisin Muffins

Ingredients:

1 1/2 cups whole wheat flour
1/2 cup ground oats
2 tsp cinnamon
1/2 tsp nutmeg
1 TBSP baking powder
1/2 tsp baking soda
1/2 tsp salt
1 can pumpkin puree
2/3 cup pure maple syrup
2/3 cup raisins

Directions:

Preheat your oven to 375 degrees. Mix together all the ingredients to form a thick batter. Pour into a lined muffin pan and bake for 25-30 minutes until golden brown.

Low Fat Coffee Cake

Ingredients:

1/4 cup vegan margarine
2 cups applesauce
1 cup flour
1 1/2 cups oat bran
1 cup splenda
1 tsp baking soda
1 tsp cinnamon
1/2 tsp nutmeg
1/4 tsp cloves
1 cup raisins
1 cup chopped walnuts

Directions:

Preheat oven to 350 degrees. Heat margarine and applesauce together in a saucepan until melted and well combined. Then pour into a large mixing bowl and stir in remaining ingredients. Pour into a greased baking pan and bake for 25-30 minutes.

Very Vegan Breakfast Casserole

Ingredients:

9 slices wheat bread, cut in cubes
1 lb soft tofu (drained and crumbled)
1 lb vegetable sausage substitute
1 red bell pepper, chopped
1 green bell pepper, chopped
1 onion, chopped
3 garlic cloves, chopped
2 cups almond milk
2 tsp thyme
2 tsp basil
2 tsp dill weed
2 tsp rosemary
1 tsp salt
1 TBSP olive oil

Directions:

Sauté onions and garlic in olive oil for 3 minutes. Add in veggie sausage and crumble. Cook until browned and then stir in peppers and cook for 5 more minutes. Remove from heat. In a 9x13 baking pan, spread out the cubed bread. Preheat oven to 350 degrees. In a mixing bowl, combine all the remaining ingredients along with the cooked vegetables and sausage.

Pour this mixture over the bread and allow to rest for 20 minutes. Bake for 40-45 minutes until evenly browned.

Easy Vegan Pancakes

Ingredients:

1 cup flour
1 TBSP sugar
2 TBSP baking powder
1/8 tsp salt
1 cup coconut milk
2 TBSP vegetable oil

Directions:

Combine the flour, sugar, baking powder and salt in a large bowl until well mixed. Add in coconut milk and beat until smooth. Drop ¼ cup batter on hot griddle and bake cook until bubbles appear on the surface of the pancake. Flip and continue cooking for 2 more minutes.

Vegan Breakfast Burrito

Ingredients:

1 tortillas
1 slice vegan cheese
1 strip extra firm tofu
2 TBSP olive oil
1 TBSP minced garlic
2 TBSP guacamole
1 TBSP salsa

Directions:

Saute tofu and garlic in olive oil for 2 minutes. Layer on top of the tortilla along with vegan cheese and microwave for 25 seconds. Top with salsa and guacamole and enjoy.

Stuffing with Cranberries

Ingredients:

2 cups toasted bread cubes
3 TBSP olive oil
1 yellow onion, diced
1/2 red onion, diced
2 stalks of celery, diced
3/4 cup cranberries, chopped
4 cups low-sodium vegetable broth
1 cup cooked wild rice
2 tsp sage
2 tsp thyme
½ cup applesauce
1 can red kidney beans, drained
Salt and pepper to taste

Directions:

Preheat oven to 375 degrees. In a large skillet, sauté onions, celery, and cranberries until soft. Add vegetable broth and bring to a boil. In a large bowl, combine toasted bread, rice, and herbs. Stir in the applesauce and the hot liquid mixture. Add beans and mix well. Pour into 2 greased 8-inch pans and cover with foil. Bake for 25 minutes and then uncover and bake 10 more minutes until top is crisp and brown.

Creamed Spinach

Ingredients:

1 TBSP cornstarch + 1 TBSP water
1 lb fresh spinach
1 cup unsweetened almond milk
1½ tsp onion powder
¼ tsp garlic powder
2 TBSP nutritional yeast
¼ tsp nutmeg
⅛ tsp pepper
1 tsp almond butter
pinch of salt

Directions:

In a small bowl or ramekin, mix cornstarch and water with a fork until uniformly combined. Set aside. In a large pot, bowl spinach until wilted. Remove from heat and drain, pressing to remove excess water. In a small pot, whisk almond milk, onion powder, and garlic and bring to a boil. Whisk continually and add in cornstarch mixture. The sauce will immediately start to thicken. Reduce heat and simmer for 2 minutes, stirring nonstop. Remove from heat and whisk in yeast, nutmeg, pepper, almond butter, and salt. Serve hot.

Roasted Carrots with Sesame Dressing

Ingredients:

1 lb carrots, peeled and chopped into small pieces
2 tsp olive oil
1 TBSP Ponzu sauce
1 tsp sesame seeds
1 TBSP chives
½ tsp sesame oil

Directions:

Roast the carrots at 375 degrees for 20-25 minutes. In a small bowl, whisk together the remaining ingredients. Toss with the cooked carrots and serve warm.

Low Fat Vegan Cheezy Sauce

Ingredients:

1 cup almond milk
¼ cup nutritional yeast
¼ tsp paprika
½ tsp miso paste
1 ½ TBSP flour
Pepper to taste

Directions:

Heat almond milk in a saucepan over medium heat. When milk is warm, sprinkle in yeast and paprika. Whisk to combine. Add in miso paste and continue whisking to break up the clumps. Gently sprinkle in flour and keep whisking. Keep heating for one or two more minutes until thickened, but stir constantly to avoid sticking or burning on the bottom. Serve as a sauce over any steamed vegetables you like.

Vegan Fried Rice

Ingredients:

1/4 cup soy sauce
3 TBSP dry white wine
2 TBSP peanut oil
2 cloves garlic, minced
1 carrot, sliced
1 green bell pepper, diced
1/2 cup green peas
4 cups pre-cooked leftover rice

Directions:

Whisk together wine and soy sauce and set aside. In a large wok, heat peanut oil and sauté garlic for one minute. Stir in the carrot, pepper, and peas. Stir fry for 2 minutes, then stir in rice. Pour soy sauce and win mixture on top of the rice and stir to combine. When the rice is hot, serve!

Santa Fe Potato Salad

Ingredients:

6-8 Yukon potatoes, cut up
3 TBSP apple cider vinegar
1/2 cup Vegan mayo
Juice from 2 limes
½ tsp cumin
1 tsp chili powder
½ cup diced red onion
1 small can green chilies, drained
½ cup cilantro, chopped
Salt and pepper to taste
2 TBSP pine nuts, toasted
Red pepper flakes to taste

Directions:

Boil potatoes until fork tender, about 20 minutes. Drain and place in a bowl. Sprinkle with vinegar, salt, and pepper. Make the dressing by mixing together Vegan mayo, lime juice, spices, onion, chilies, and cilantro. Mix dressing into the potatoes and add in cilantro and toasted pine nuts. Fold together to combine. Chill for 1 hour before serving.

Spicy Creole Cole Slaw

Ingredients:

1/2 head green cabbage, shredded
1/2 head purple cabbage, shredded
2 carrots, grated
1 red onion, diced
3 green onions, diced
1 red chili pepper, minced
1 1/2 cups Vegan mayo
3 TBSP Dijon mustard
2 TBSP creole seasoning
1 TBSP apple cider vinegar
2 TBSP lemon juice
dash sugar
dash hot sauce, to taste
salt and pepper to taste

Directions:

In a large bowl, toss together the cabbage, carrots, onions and chili pepper. In a separate small bowl, whisk together the vegan mayonnaise, mustard, creole seasoning, vinegar, lemon juice and sugar. Pour this mixture over the cabbage mix, and gently toss to coat. Add a dash of hot sauce, salt and pepper, and chill for at least one hour before serving.

Greek Stuffed Eggplant

Ingredients:

4 medium eggplants
1 cup vegetable broth
1 large red onion, diced
5 large cloves of garlic, minced
4 cups of fresh tomatoes, diced
1 1/2 cups cooked brown rice
Juice from ½ lemon
2 tsp oregano
1/2 cup parsley, chopped
3 tsp maple syrup
½ tsp salt
Pepper to taste

Directions:

Cap eggplants and slice in half. Bring a large pot of water to a boil and boil eggplant skin side down for 15 minutes. Depending on how large your pot is, you may have to boil 4 halves at a time. Once they are boiled, set aside to cool. Preheat oven to 350 degrees. Scoop out eggplant from shell and leave behind a small layer of flesh to keep skin from tearing. Heat up a large wok and sauté onions in vegetable broth for 5 minutes.

Mash up the eggplant pulp and add in tomatoes and onions and continue cooking. Add cooked rice, parsley, oregano, lemon juice, and salt and pepper to eggplant and tomatoes. Place the eggplants shells skin side down on a lined baking sheet and fill with tomato eggplant mixture. Bake for 20 minutes or until heated through.

Stuffed Golden Squash

Ingredients:

4 small winter squashes
2/3 cup raw millet
1 large red onion, chopped
2 cloves garlic, minced
1/2 red bell pepper, diced
2 TBSP wheat germ
Juice from 1 orange
1 tsp cumin
1/2 tsp turmeric
Salt and pepper
Paprika for topping

Directions:

Cut the squashes in half lengthwise. Place the halves in a baking dish, cut side up, with about 1/4 inch of water on the bottom, and cover. Bake at 375 degrees for 30 to 45 minutes. Allow the squashes to cool and then scoop out and seeds and discard. Scoop out the pulp leaving about ½ inch shell all around to keep skin from tearing. Chop the pulp up and place in a bowl. Set aside. Boil millet for 35 millets. Saute onion, garlic, and pepper. Add in the cooked millet, orange juice, wheat germ, chopped up squash pulp and seasonings. Stir together.

Stuff each squash with millet mixture and sprinkle with wheat germ and paprika on top. Cover with foil and bake for 25 minutes. Uncover and bake 15 more minutes.

Mexican Green Rice

Ingredients:

1 1/2 cups medium grain white rice
½ cup cilantro
½ cup parsley
2 cloves garlic, coarsely chopped
1/4 cup olive oil
1 1/2 tsp sea salt

Directions:

Cook the rice according to package directions. In your food processor, combine the herbs, garlic, and olive oil. Process until thoroughly pureed. Just before serving, stir the herb mixture and salt into the rice.

Stuffed Baked Potatoes

Ingredients:

2 TBSP Mrs. Dash Original Blend
2 baked potatoes (still warm)
2 TBSP olive oil
¼ cup chopped red onion
1 celery stalk, chopped

Directions:

Preheat oven to 350 degrees. Slice potatoes in half and scoop out pulp and reserve in a bowl. Saute onions and celery in olive oil. Then toss in the potato pulp and Mrs. Dash. Mix together and stuff in potato skins. Bake for 10 minutes.

Vegan Mashed Potatoes

Ingredients:

6 large potatoes, diced
1 cup cashew cream
3 TBSP vegan margarine
1/4 cup chopped fresh chives
salt and pepper, to taste

Directions:

Place the potatoes in a large pot and cover with water. Bring to a boil and cook for 20 minutes. Drain the potatoes, place in a bowl with the remaining ingredients, and mix until smooth. Serve hot.

Roasted Hot Potatoes

Ingredients:

1 pound small red potatoes
2 TBSP olive oil
salt and pepper to taste
2 TBSP rosemary

Directions:

Quarter potatoes and place on a greased baking sheet. Drizzle with olive oil and season with salt, pepper, and rosemary. Bake at 425 degrees for 25-35 minutes.

Apple Celery Cole Slaw

Ingredients:

½ head of cabbage, chopped or a bag of cole slaw mix
1 granny smith apple, cored and chopped
1 celery stalk, chopped
½ small yellow onion, chopped
¼ cup olive oil
1 tsp celery seed
2 TBSP lemon juice
2 TBSP raw honey

Directions:

Combine cabbage, apple, celery, and onion in a large bowl. In a separate bowl, whisk together remaining ingredients and then pour over the slaw mixture and toss to coat.

Zucchini Pasta Salad

Ingredients:

5 medium sized zucchinis
5 cherry tomatoes, halved
1 cup pitted black olives, chopped
1 TBSP balsamic vinegar
1 TBSP olive oil
2 tsp salt

Directions:

Use a peeler to create long julienne strips of zucchini. Sprinkle with 2 tsp salt and allow to sit for 20 minutes. The salt will pull a lot of moisture from the zucchini strips, making them have a noodle consistency. Drain your zucchini with a colander and then wash them thoroughly to remove excess salt. Squeeze the strips to get out all the excess moisture. Drizzle olive oil and vinegar over your noodles and the add in tomato an olives. Toss to combine and enjoy a Paleo version of pasta salad.

Cajun Carrot Crisps

Ingredients:

10 carrots, peeled and cut into thin slices like French fries
1 TBSP olive oil
salt and pepper to taste

Directions:

Preheat oven to 450 degrees. While it is heating, toss your carrot slices with oil. Spray a baking sheet with nonstick spray and arrange your carrot sticks in a single layer. Sprinkle lightly with salt and pepper. Bake for 15 minutes; then flip carrots over and bake an additional 10 minutes or until crisp.

Chili Lime Sweet Potato Chips

Ingredients:

2 sweet potatoes, peeled and sliced thin with a mandolin
2 TBSP olive oil
Garlic salt
Chili powder
2 limes cut in wedges

Directions:

Preheat oven to 400 degrees. Arrange sweet potato slices on a parchment lined baking sheet coated with nonstick spray. Drizzle with olive oil and then sprinkle with garlic salt and chili powder. Bake for 15 minutes; then flip the slices over. Bake an additional 10 minutes or until crisp and beginning to brown. Spritz with lime before serving.

Roasted Artichoke Hearts

Ingredients:

3 (15 ounce) cans artichoke hearts
4 cloves of garlic, quartered
2 tsp olive oil
Salt and pepper to taste
Juice from ½ lemon

Directions:

Preheat oven to 375°F. Drain the artichokes and rinse in a colander. Next, mix the artichokes with olive oil and garlic and toss to combine. Pour the mixture on a baking sheet and roast for one hour, turning every 20 minutes. Sprinkle with salt, pepper, and lemon juice before serving.

Beet Fries

Ingredients:

3 red beets
1/2 tsp olive oil
1/4 cup diced green onion
2 cloves of garlic, minced
1/4 tsp sea salt

Directions:

Preheat oven to 425 degrees and line a baking sheet with parchment paper. Rinse and peel beets and cut in strips about ½ inch wide. Toss the beets with olive oil and remaining ingredients then spread on the baking sheet and bake for 25 minutes, flipped them over halfway through.

Broccoli Slaw

Ingredients:

1/2 cup broccoli florets, cut small
2 broccoli stems, peeled
2 carrots, peeled
1 TBSP poppy seeds
1/3 cup Vegan mayo
1 granny smith apple, peeled, cored and diced

Directions:

Grate the broccoli stems and carrots. Place in a bowl and combine with remaining ingredients. Stir everything together and then chill in the refrigerator for at least one hour before serving.

Ginger Glazed Carrots

Ingredients:

2 lb baby carrots
3 TBSP olive oil
3 TBSP pure maple syrup
1/2 tsp ginger

Directions:

Preheat oven to 350 degrees. Wash and peel the carrots and arrange them on a baking sheet. Drizzle with olive oil and maple syrup, then sprinkle ginger on top. Bake for 10-15 minutes.

Collard Greens

Ingredients:

3 TBSP olive oil
1 cup diced tomato
1 yellow onion, diced
2 cloves garlic, minced
2 lbs collard greens, stems removed
2 TBSP thyme
salt and pepper to taste

Directions:

In a large, non-stick skillet, heat oil and sauté tomatoes over low heat. Add onions and garlic, cooking until onions are translucent. Add greens, cover and steam for 10 minutes. Add salt, pepper and thyme and cover for an additional 15 minutes to continue to steam or until the greens are wilted but not soggy. Serve warm with vinegar on the side.

Lentil Shepherds Pie

Ingredients:

1/2 pound lentils, cooked and drained
1 onion, diced
1/2 tsp crumbled fresh sage
1/2 tsp minced garlic
pinch of dried oregano
1 tsp salt
dash cayenne pepper
3 large potatoes, cooked
1/2 to 1 cup of hot almond milk
margarine to taste

Directions:

Pre-heat the oven to 400 degrees. In a large mixing bowl, mash the cooked lentils thoroughly and add the onion and seasonings. Put the lentil mixture in a lightly oiled casserole dish. In a separate bowl, mash the potatoes and add the hot almond milk, margarine and salt. Beat by hand or with an electric mixer until fluffy. Spread the mashed potatoes on top of the mashed lentils and bake for 20 minutes or until the potatoes are dry on top. Place the pie under the broiler to brown on top. Serve warm.

Asparagus Stir Fry

Ingredients:

Toasted sesame oil
8 oz. extra firm tofu, sliced
4 green onions (thinly sliced)
1 TBSP grated ginger
1/2 tsp crushed red pepper flakes
1 bunch asparagus, trimmed and cut to 1-inch pieces
1 tsp salt
3 cloves garlic, minced
1 handful cashews, chopped
3 handfuls kale, chopped
1 lime
2 TBSP hoisin sauce
1 handful mint, diced
1 handful basil, diced

Directions:

Heat the sesame oil in a large pan over medium high heat. When it is hot, add the tofu, and cook until golden. Remove the tofu from the pan and set aside. Add another splash of oil to the pan and, as soon as it is hot, add the onions, ginger, red pepper flakes, asparagus, and salt.

Stir fry for about a minute, then add the garlic, cashews, and kale and stir-fry for another minute, or until the kale wilts. Return the tofu to the pan. Stir in the lime zest and juice and the hoisin sauce. Cook for another 10-20 seconds, stirring all the while. Remove from heat and stir in the mint and basil. Taste and add a bit more salt if needed.

Vegan Macaroni and Cheese

Ingredients:

1/4 cup water
1/2 of a 10.5 oz. box of firm or firm lite silken tofu
1/4 cup nutritional yeast flakes
1 – 2 oz jar pimentos
1/2 tsp liquid smoke
1 1/2 tsp seasoned rice vinegar
3/4 tsp salt
1/2 tsp garlic powder
1/4 tsp onion powder
1/2 tsp vegetarian Worcestershire sauce
1/2 tsp soy sauce

Directions:

Boil the noodles. Combine remaining ingredients in blender and puree. Drain noodles; toss with sauce to serve.

Indian Cauliflower Curry

Ingredients:

1 1/2 tsp fresh ginger, grated
2 TBSP sesame seeds
3 TBSP peanuts
3 cloves garlic, minced
1 TBSP cumin
1 tsp ground cloves
1 tsp turmeric
1/2 tsp cayenne pepper
2 TBSP water
1 TBSP olive oil
2 onions, diced
1 head of cauliflower, chopped
Juice from ½ lemon

Directions:

In a blender, combine ginger, sesame seeds, peanuts, garlic, spices and water. Saute the onions in olive oil over medium high heat about 3-5 minutes, or until onions turn clear. Add cauliflower and spices mixture and cover. Allow to cook another 10-12 minutes, stirring occasionally until cauliflower is almost done. Add lemon juice and allow to cook for 3 more minutes.

Avocado Pesto Pasta

Ingredients:

4 ripe avocados, peeled and pitted
3 1/2 cups fresh basil
1 cup olive oil
1 ½ cup almonds
Juice from 1 lemon
2 cloves of garlic, minced
1 tsp salt

Directions:

Place all ingredients in a blender and puree until smooth. Heat up in a saucepan and serve over boiled pasta of your choice.

Vegan Bean Taco Filling

Ingredients:

1 TBSP olive oil
1 onion, diced
2 cloves garlic, minced
1 bell pepper, chopped
2 cans black beans, rinsed, drained, and mashed
2 TBSP cornmeal
1 1/2 TBSP cumin
1 tsp paprika
1 tsp cayenne pepper
1 tsp chili powder
1 cup salsa

Directions:

Heat olive oil in a medium skillet over medium heat. Stir in onion, garlic, and bell pepper; cook until tender. Stir in mashed beans. Add the cornmeal. Mix in cumin, paprika, cayenne, chili powder, and salsa. Cover, and cook 5 minutes.

Mushroom Stroganoff

Ingredients:

2 TBSP cornstarch
3 TBSP soy sauce
1 1/ 3 cups vegetable broth
1/ 2 tsp garlic granules
3 TBSP tahini
2 cups thinly sliced onions
4 cloves garlic, minced or pressed
4 cups sliced fresh mushrooms
2 cups thinly sliced seitan strips
Salt and Pepper to taste

Directions:

To make the gravy, place the cornstarch and soy sauce in a saucepan and stir them together well to make a thin, smooth paste. Gradually whisk in the vegetable broth and garlic granules. Continue cooking until it thickens and comes to a boil. Remove the saucepan from the heat and whisk in tahini. Cover the saucepan with a lid, and set it aside. Heat a large, non-stick skillet over medium-high heat. Add the onions and garlic, and sauté them for 10 minutes, adding water if necessary to prevent sticking.

Add the mushrooms to the onion in the skillet and cook, stirring often, for 5 more minutes. Stir in seitan strips and the reserved gravy into the onion and mushrooms in the skillet. Reduce the heat to low and cook, stirring often, about 5 more minutes just until the seitan is heated through. Season with pepper and serve.

Mexican Vegan Lasagna

Ingredients:

2 large sweet potatoes
1 can of black beans
1 small white onion
5 corn tortillas
1 can of green chile enchilada sauce
1/2 TBSP chile powder
1/2 TBSP cumin
1/2 tsp cayenne pepper
1/4 cup nutritional yeast

Directions:

Preheat oven to 375 degrees. Peel and cube sweet potatoes. Toss potatoes with chile powder. Spread across baking sheet and bake for 35 min. or until tender when poked with fork. Rinse black beans with water and put in sweet potato bowl. Toss with cumin and cayenne pepper. Sauté onion in non-stick pan until translucent. Once potatoes are done, reduce oven to 350. Cut corn tortillas in halves and quarters to aid with layering. Layer lasagna in 8×8 baking dish as follows: green chile sauce, tortillas, black beans, sweet potatoes, onions. Once all ingredients are used up (mine makes 2 layers) top with nutritional yeast.

Cover with foil and bake for at 350 degrees for 25 minutes. Uncover and bake for 20 minutes longer.

Asian Ginger Noodles

Ingredients:

4 cups vegetable broth
2 oz. fresh ginger, peeled and thinly sliced
8 oz. firm tofu, cubed
2 cups broccoli
4 oz. dried soba noodles
2 TBSP soy sauce
1/4 cup fresh basil, shredded
1/8 cup fresh mint, shredded
Juice of ½ lime
Crushed Red Pepper Flakes to taste

Directions:

Place the broth, ginger and tofu in a large saucepan and bring to a boil. Turn down the heat, and simmer for 10 minutes. Remove (just) the tofu from the pan using a slotted spoon and set aside. Now add the broccoli to the simmering broth. Cook for just a minute, until bright, and remove from pan with fork. Add pasta to ginger broth and cook until done, stirring regularly. Remove pasta with fork, set aside, and pour out most of the broth and all of the ginger slices. Return the tofu, broccoli and noodles to the pot.

Stir in the soy sauce, basil, mint, and lime juice. Finish with a couple pinches of crushed red pepper flakes.

Belizean Coconut Curry

Ingredients:

½ tsp grated ginger
5 cloves garlic
1 onion
2 stalks fresh lemongrass
3 TBSP olive oil
Red pepper flakes to taste
1 block tofu, drained and cubed
1 1/2 TBSP curry powder
2 cups coconut milk
1 cup water

Directions:

In a blender, combine ginger, garlic, onion and lemongrass until smooth, adding a bit of olive oil if needed. Heat the olive oil in a large skillet over medium-high heat and add the blended garlic mixture. Saute this mixture for 1-3 minutes, then add the tofu and red pepper flakes, stirring gently to mix the tofu with the garlic mixture for another 3-5 minutes, adding more olive oil if needed. Reduce heat to medium low and add coconut, water, and curry, stirring well to combine.

Cover the skillet and allow to simmer for 20 minutes, stirring occasionally.

Cheezy Tortilla Pizza

Ingredients:

2 tortillas
2 cups cooked black beans
1/3 cup vegan cheezy sauce
3 TBSP minced parsley
½ cup chopped red onion
½ cup chopped bell pepper
½ chopped avocado
¼ tsp salt
pizza sauce
Sprinkle of non-dairy cheese

Directions:

Preheat oven to 350 degrees. In a medium bowl, mix together beans, cheezy sauce, parsley, onion, pepper, and seasonings. Place tortillas on a baking sheet and top with pizza sauce. Put bean mixture on top. Sprinkle on dairy-free cheese. Bake at 350 degrees for 10 minutes.

Tomato Barley Risotto

Ingredients:

1 cup dry pot barley
1 TBSP olive oil
½ tsp oregano
½ tsp basil
1 garlic clove, minced
1 ½ cups diced tomatoes
1 cup almond milk
½ cup water
¼ cup yeast
½ TBSP miso mixed with ½ TBSP water
Salt to taste

Directions:

Rinse pot barley in a strainer and place into medium sized pot that has a lid. Add olive oil, basil, and oregano and stir well until barley is coated with oil. Turn heat to medium until barley begins to sizzle. Once the barley sizzles, add in the minced garlic and reduce heat to low-medium. Cook for 1 minute and then add in the tomatoes, milk, water, nutritional yeast, miso, and salt. Stir well and bring to a gentle boil and then cover and reduce heat to low.

Cook, covered (with a bit of air escaping) for 30-35 minutes, stirring every 5 minutes or so, being careful not to burn the barley on the bottom of the pot. The mixture should be creamy, but not soupy, and the barley will be very chewy and not mushy. Serve immediately.

Coconut Mint Pudding

Ingredients:

2 cups coconut meat
1 cup almond milk
1 TBSP mint extract
¼ cup almond butter
1 TBSP chia seeds
4 TBSP coconut sugar

Directions:

Place all ingredients in the blender and puree until smooth. Chill for 2-3 hours before serving.

Caribbean Breeze Ice Cream

Ingredients:

4 cups of coconut milk
1 ¾ cups sugar
2 tsp vanilla extract

Directions:

Chill the coconut milk and then pour it in the blender. Add in sugar and vanilla and blend until smooth. Pour the liquid into an ice cream machine or in the freezer.

Raspberry Chocolate Shake

Ingredients:

1 ½ cups almond milk
1 cup frozen raspberries
1 or 2 chocolate truffles
2 pitted dates
1 tsp cinnamon

Directions:

Place all the ingredients in a blender and puree on high until smooth and creamy.

Vegan Gingerbread Cake

Ingredients:

2 TBSP ground flax seeds
6 TBSP warm water
2 cups flour
¼ cup potato starch
1 tsp baking powder
1 tsp baking soda
2 tsp ginger
1 tsp cinnamon
¼ tsp ground cloves
¼ tsp salt
2/3 cup coconut sugar
½ cup molasses
1/3 cup coconut oil
1 cup applesauce

Directions:

Preheat oven toe 350 degrees. Grease an 8x8-inch pan or line it with parchment paper. In a small bowl, stir together the flax and warm water until the mixture is thick and creamy. Set aside for at least 10 minutes. Sift the dry ingredients (except the coconut palm sugar) into a large mixing bowl.

In another mixing bowl, combine the coconut palm sugar, molasses, coconut oil, applesauce, and flax mixture; whisk until well blended. Add to the dry ingredients and stir to blend. Pour the batter into the prepared pan. Bake until set in the middle and a tester comes out clean, about 35 minutes. Cool in pan on rack until cake is cool enough to handle, then turn out.

Vegan Chocolate Cake

Ingredients:

1 1/2 cups flour
1 cup white sugar
1/4 cup cocoa powder
1 tsp baking soda
1/2 tsp salt
1/3 cup vegetable oil
1 tsp vanilla extract
1 tsp white vinegar
1 cup water

Directions:

Preheat oven to 350 degrees. Sift together the flour, sugar, cocoa, baking soda and salt. Add the oil, vanilla, vinegar and water. Mix together until smooth. Pour into a 9x9 cake pan and bake for 45 minutes.

Sweet Mexican Nachos

Ingredients:

4 flour tortillas
2 TBSP vegan margarine, melted
1 TBSP cinnamon
1 TBSP sugar

Directions:

Slice the flour tortillas like a pizza into 6 slices. Drizzle with melted margarine and then sprinkle with cinnamon and sugar. Bake at 350 degrees for about ten minutes or until crispy.

Moroccan Orange Dessert

Ingredients:

3-4 oranges
¼ cup orange flower water
2 TBSP powdered sugar
2 tsp cinnamon

Directions:

Slice the top and bottom off each orange. Slice off the rind and all the pith and then cut the orange into 1/4 inch rounds. Sprinkle a little orange flower water in the bottom of a wide-bottomed glass or plastic container and lay the orange slices on top. If you need to do more than one layer of oranges to get them all in the container, sprinkle more orange flower water over each orange layer as you go. Add any remaining orange flower water, cover the container and set aside at room temperature for 1 hour. Before serving, sprinkle with powdered sugar and cinnamon.

Chocolate Pudding

Ingredients:

½ cup raw cashews, soaked
¼ cup unsweetened almond milk
1 large sweet potato
1 cup canned coconut milk
1 ½ TBSP chia seeds
1-3 drops stevia
½ cup dark vegan chocolate chips

Directions:

Soak the raw cashews in water in a well-covered container for 6 hours or longer. Drain water, rinse cashews and set aside. Preheat oven to 325 degrees. Wash and pierce the sweet potato with a fork and wrap in foil. Place on a baking tray and bake in the oven for 45 minutes or until tender. Allow to cool for 15 minutes. Mash and place the warm sweet potato, stevia, coconut milk, almond milk and soaked cashews into your blender, pulsing until you have a thick, creamy consistency. Transfer ingredients to a glass bowl. Allow mixture to cool and stir in chia seeds and chocolate chunks. Refrigerated covered for 4-6 hours before serving.

Carob Pudding

Ingredients:

1 TBSP tahini
1 cup water
3 TBSP carob
1 TBSP instant coffee
1 tsp vanilla
7 prunes
1 large date, pitted

Directions:

In a blender, blend all ingredients on high until smooth. Chill for 2 hours before serving.

Vegan Chocolate Chip Cookies

Ingredients:

2 1/2 cups all-purpose flour
1 tsp baking
1 tsp salt
2 sticks margarine
1 ¼ cups sugar
1 TBSP molasses
2 tsp vanilla extract
1 1/2 cups vegan semisweet chocolate chips

Directions:

Heat the oven to 350 degrees and position rack in the middle. Place the flour, baking soda, and salt in a medium bowl and whisk together until smooth. Place the margarine and sugar in a mixer and beat on medium-high speed until light and fluffy, about 3 minutes. Scrape down the sides of the bowl. Add the molasses and vanilla and beat on medium-high speed until combined, about 2 minutes. Add the flour mixture and beat on low speed until just combined. Fold in chocolate chips. Drop by spoonfuls onto baking sheet and bake for 8-11 minutes.

Cranberry Walnut Chocolate Truffles

Ingredients:

¾ cup walnuts
1 cup cocoa powder
⅛ tsp salt
1 tsp ground cinnamon
2 tsp vanilla extract
1 cup maple syrup
¼ cup melted coconut oil
1/2 cup dried cranberries

Directions:

Place walnuts in a food processor and pulse to chop. Place the nuts in a shallow dish to roll your truffles later. Clean food processor and then add remaining ingredients except cranberries, pulsing until a batter forms. Fold in cranberries and cover and freeze for two hours. Scoop out truffles with a melon baller and roll in walnuts. Cover and freeze for 1 hour before serving.

Carob Cake

Ingredients:

3 cups almond meal
1 cup raw honey
5 TBSP carob powder
1 tsp sea salt
1/4 cup applesauce
1/2 cup water

Directions:

Mix all ingredients together the pour in a greased cake pan. Bake for half an hour at 350 degrees. Store in the refrigerator overnight and the next morning, they have the consistency of brownies!

Fig and Almond Bites

Ingredients:

2 cups almond meal
1 cup soft dried figs, hard tips removed
2 tsp finely grated orange zest
1 tsp vanilla extract
1/2 tsp salt

Directions:

Preheat oven to 325 degrees. In a food processor, blend together the almond meal, figs, orange zest, vanilla, and salt. The mixture will resemble the texture of wet sand when it is ready. Form dough into small balls and place on a greased baking sheet about ½ inch apart. Bake for 12-15 minutes or until the bottoms of your cookies are lightly browned.

Chocolate Almond Butter Fudge

Ingredients:

2 TBSP almond butter
2 TBSP coconut butter
2 TBSP cocoa powder
½ very ripe banana
1/8 tsp salt
1 tsp raw honey

Directions:

Combine all ingredients in a food processor and pulse to mix. Scoop out and press into a cake pan. Refrigerate until firm.

The Ultimate Hot Chocolate

Ingredients:

1 cup coconut milk
2 TBSP coconut powder
1/16 tsp salt
1 TBSP raw honey

Directions:

Combine all the ingredients in a saucepan and whisk together over low heat. Bring to a simmer and then pour your hot chocolate in a large mug and enjoy.

Simply Divine Chocolate Mousse

Ingredients:

1 cup coconut milk
1 cup dates, pitted
1 tsp vanilla extract
5 oz. dark chocolate

Directions:

Set the coconut milk in a cool place overnight and allow the cream and water to separate. Scoop the cream off the top and place it in a food processor with your dates and pulse until smooth. Press the mixture through a fine mesh sieve to remove any date skins and insure a smooth texture. Melt the chocolate over low heat and stir into the coconut milk mixture. Add in vanilla. Spoon your finished mousse into ramekins and chill until firm. Serve with a topping of whipped coconut milk.

Warm Honey Walnut Dressing

Ingredients:

2 tablespoons peanut oil
1/4 cup chopped walnuts
1/3 cup honey
1/4 cup maple syrup
1/2 cup bottled Italian dressing
1 can sweet dark pitted cherries, drained

Directions:

Whisk together ingredients and then heat in a saucepan. Drizzle over salad while warm for a sweet twist of your usual salad.

Vegan French Dressing

Ingredients:

1 can condensed tomato soup
1 cup vegetable oil
3/4 cup apple cider vinegar
1 small onion, grated
1/4 cup sugar
1 clove garlic, minced
1 tablespoon Dijon mustard
1 tablespoon horseradish, optional
1 teaspoon salt
1 teaspoon black pepper

Directions:

Mix all ingredients together in a large bowl. Chill for 1 hour before serving.

Fast Southwest Dressing

Ingredients:

1 cup picante sauce
1 cup cashew cream
1/4 teaspoon chili powder
1/4 teaspoon ground cumin

Directions:

Mix all ingredients together in a large bowl. Chill for 1 hour before serving.

Honey Poppy Seed Dressing

Ingredients:

3/4 cup vegan mayonnaise
1/3 cup honey
2 tablespoons yellow mustard
2 tablespoons poppy seeds
1/8 teaspoon salt
1/8 teaspoon black pepper

Directions:

Mix all ingredients together in a large bowl. Chill for 1 hour before serving.

60-Second Vinaigrette Dressing

Ingredients:

1 cup olive oil
1/4 cup white vinegar
1 teaspoon garlic powder
1 teaspoon onion powder
1 teaspoon salt
1/2 teaspoon black pepper

Directions:

Whisk together all ingredients in a small bowl and serve immediately.

Classic Dijon Dressing

Ingredients:

1 cup vegetable oil
1/2 cup cider vinegar
3/4 teaspoon salt
1 tablespoon Dijon mustard
1 tablespoon grated onion
1 tablespoon sugar

Directions:

Whisk together all ingredients and chill for one hour before serving.

Blueberry Twist Dressing

Ingredients:

1 cup fresh or frozen blueberries, thawed, divided
1/4 cup vegetable oil
2 tablespoons orange marmalade
2 teaspoons lemon juice
1 teaspoon Dijon mustard
1/4 teaspoon salt

Directions:

Place all ingredients in a blender and pulse until smooth. Use immediately.

Double Garlic Dressing

Ingredients:

2/3 cup white vinegar
1/2 cup olive or vegetable oil
1/4 cup water
4 garlic cloves, minced
1 teaspoon garlic powder
1 1/2 teaspoons salt
1 teaspoon black pepper

Directions:

Place all ingredients in a medium bowl and whisk to combine. Serve immediately.

Tahini Dill Sauce

Ingredients:

¼ cup fresh lemon juice
3 tablespoons Tahini
3 tablespoons water
1 tablespoon chopped fresh dill
Pinch cayenne pepper
salt and pepper, to taste

Directions:

Whisk all ingredients together.

Summer Lemon Vinaigrette

Ingredients:

3 tablespoon fresh lemon juice
3 tablespoons olive oil
salt and pepper, to taste

Directions:

Whisk all ingredients together.

Creamy Carrot Apple Sauce

Ingredients:

½ pound carrots, peeled and grated
1 granny smith apple, peeled and chopped
¼ cup cider vinegar
½ cup vegetable oil
2 tablespoons water
salt, to taste

Directions:

Place everything in a blender and puree all ingredients together until smooth.

Green Heaven Dressing

Ingredients:

1 cup baby spinach
½ cup cashew cream
½ avocado
¼ cup fresh tarragon leaves, chopped
Juice from ½ lemon
1 small clove garlic
salt and black pepper, to taste
water

Directions:

Blend together the first 7 ingredients in a food processor or blender. Add as much water as you need to thin until you achieve the desired consistency.

Citrus Chives Dressing

Ingredients:

¼ cup olive oil
1 shallot, minced
2 tablespoons good quality red wine vinegar
1 tablespoon chopped parsley
Juice and zest of 1 orange
salt and black pepper, to taste

Directions:

Cook the shallots in the oil until soft. Let cool. In a bowl combine the shallot mixture with the remaining ingredients.

Asian Honey Glaze

Ingredients:

3 TBSP honey
1 ½ TBSP rice wine vinegar
1/3 cup vegan mayo
1 tsp Dijon mustard
1/8 tsp sesame oil

Directions:

Whisk together all ingredients until smooth.

Ginger Vinaigrette

Ingredients:

1/4 cup(s) rice vinegar
1 1/2 tablespoon(s) sugar
1 tablespoon(s) finely grated fresh ginger
1/4 cup(s) vegetable oil
Kosher salt and freshly ground pepper

Directions:

Mix together all ingredients and chill for 1 hour.

Italian Basil Vinaigrette

Ingredients:

1 small garlic clove
1 cup basil leaves, chopped
1/4 cup(s) extra-virgin olive oil
1 TBSP white vinegar
Pinch of crushed red pepper
Salt and freshly ground black pepper

Directions:

Mix together all ingredients and chill for 1 hour.

Citrus Honey Dressing

Ingredients:

1 tablespoon(s) plus 2 teaspoons fresh lemon juice
1 teaspoon(s) finely grated lemon zest
1 tablespoon(s) honey
1/2 teaspoon(s) chopped thyme
1/4 cup(s) extra-virgin olive oil
Kosher salt and freshly ground pepper

Directions:

Mix together all ingredients and chill for 1 hour.

Garlic Lime Salad Dressing

Ingredients:

1/4 tsp kosher sea salt
1 tsp garlic, finely minced
2 tsp shallots, minced
Juice from 2 limes
1 cup extra-virgin olive oil
Salt and pepper to taste

Directions:

Whisk all ingredients together in a small bowl. Add additional lime juice or olive oil until you reach the desired balance of flavors.

Pineapple Fruit Salad Dressing

Ingredients:

1/3 cup olive oil
1/4 cup lemon juice
1/2 cup pineapple juice
2 TBSP raw honey
Zest from ½ lemon and ½ orange

Directions:

Put all ingredients in a blender and pulse until well combined. Pour over any fresh fruit salad or over a salad of mixed greens for a sweet twist.

Russian Dressing

Ingredients:

1 cup whole canned tomatoes
1/2 cup olive oil
Juice from 2 lemons
1 TBSP raw honey
1 tsp paprika
1 green onion, chopped
1 garlic clove
1 tsp horseradish powder

Directions:

Place all ingredients in a blender and pulse until well combined.

Cilantro Aioli

Ingredients:

1/3 cup fresh cilantro
Juice and zest from ½ lime
3 drops of hot sauce
1 tsp ground cumin
3/4 cup Vegan mayo

Directions:

Add all ingredients to a blender and mix until well combined and a thick, creamy consistency.

Vegan Ranch Dressing

Ingredients:

½ cup vegan mayo
½ cup almond milk
1 TBSP dill
1 tsp garlic powder
Salt and pepper to taste

Directions:

Add all ingredients to a blender and mix to combine. Taste and adjust seasoning as necessary. Keep refrigerated for up to one week. This is delicious on a salad or as a dip with vegetables.

Tartar Sauce

Ingredients:

1 cup Vegan mayo
½ cup yellow onion, diced
1 TBSP lemon juice
½ tsp dried dill

Directions:

Mix ingredients thoroughly and then refrigerate for at least one hour before serving.

Maple Tahini Dressing

Ingredients:

2 TBSP tahini
2 TBSP maple syrup
3 TBSP lemon juice
2 TBSP olive oil
salt, pepper, garlic, and cayenne to taste

Directions:

Whisk together all ingredients until smooth and serve over a green salad.

Creamy Curry Dressing

Ingredients:

1 TBSP maple syrup
1 TBSP tahini
1 tsp hot curry powder
2 tsp lemon juice
1 tsp cayenne pepper

Directions:

Mix all ingredients together until creamy and smooth.

Printed in Dunstable, United Kingdom

79273414R00088